LOST ON MEMORY LANE

What I learned when Mom was unable to

Lost on Memory Lane

By

Rodney A Drury

Published by Redneck Mystic Media

Published by Redneck Mystic Media
3011 N. Delaware St.

Peoria IL 61603

ISBN
978-1-942421-18-4

CONTENTS

FORWARD

Empathy is a difficult thing to grapple
with. Empathy requires understanding
and relationship. Empathy requires
vulnerability to feel what another
person feels. My time as a case
manager has taught me that empathy
is the necessary connection between
people--a connection that provides a
safe space for change, exploration,
and sharing of hurt. Not all situations
are easy to empathize with, especially
when they are outside of our own
personal experiences. When loved
ones are faced with a diagnosis that
steals their mind it can be very
difficult to remain empathetic. My
husband's grandmother currently
experiences dementia and rarely

recognizes family members. However, sing a hymn and she can immediately sing along. Yet, beyond hymn singing, who can relate to an adult in body with the mind of a child? I would recommend this book because it helps to bridge that gap. Rod, my dad, has always been able to empathize with others. In this book, I believe he takes that empathy a step farther and brings in understanding. Our hearts break when loved ones can't remember who they are or who we are to them. Sometimes, we buckle under the disconnect between what a person is now and what they once were. Reading this book is an experience full of humor, relationship, and heart. This book is for everyone, but especially for those who have loved ones that may no longer seem to be themselves. Rod has written this book out of the love for my Grandma, and out of that love I am encouraged to take a different perspective, a loving perspective, because you never know what another person is struggling with. Love truly is the force that heals and brings hope. May you enjoy this book as much as I did. May you develop a new way to listen as you read.

Amelia Melton

SNAPSHOT AND INSIGHT

I have an old trunk full of trophies, pictures, news articles and snapshots of my sporting achievements. It's nice to investigate that old box now and then to remember the times when success was as easy as winning a wrestling match or recovering a fumble on the football field. If I linger long enough, I can sometimes stir up the old emotions that were present when the artifact was obtained.

I can remember the auditorium filled with people applauding when some tournament was won or some award given. The hours of work and sacrifice seemed to diminish when you climbed the podium, smiled for the photos and shared your insights into victory.

I haven't climbed a podium for years. I don't think my sister ever has.

But somehow Sue has endured, sacrificed and won the victory. She has, without the energy of a cheering auditorium or the praise of a crowd, won the battle of love and care. And she is not alone. Caregivers all over this country, all over the world win, with little to no ovation or recognition.

My little brother Jon has gone to the loving aid of sister and mom. I have done it once. It was an eye-opening experience. One that so touched my life that I wish I could build a place for Sue and Jon and givers of care to climb up in front of a crowd of cheering people and receive a little love for the love they have given. I know that even if I never make that place in society, I already have built that place in my heart.

In the imagery of snapshots and insights I write this book. I wanted to capture a moment in the wrestling match when a move was made creating a need to be countered. That is the "snapshot." The "insight" is my attempt to help the caregiver respond well.

But I also hope all who read these words will also hear my spirit cheering them on. Not because the match they face is to win some trophies or even praise, but because they are wrestling for humanity. They are people who show us how people, how human kind should be, can be. They are a message to our world and to our soul that people matter. Some of us say it. These unknown and un-applauded givers live it.

Thank You.

EMPATHY

"the ability to understand and share the feelings of another"

Personally, I need to work at empathy. It doesn't come easy. I know that understanding and connecting with people matters. It matters to me. I want to be

5

understood. I want to know that people are listening.

So, during a time of care for my mom with dementia, I had to find a way to keep myself focused. I needed a way to remind myself to be empathetic, to care, and to listen. I tasked myself with trying to discover her perspective and translate that into a short saying that I could ponder. It was my way of dealing with myself and seeking to understand Mom.

I wasn't trying to understand what Mom was saying as much as understand where Mom was. What was she living in that I didn't know? This quest for knowledge has been a lifelong friend. My most favorite quote is, "you don't know what you don't know." You may have other drives. Maybe you are more motivated by love, or by comforting people. I hope this book helps people connect with those battling dementia regardless of their foundational motivations.

Most of the time we treat people differently if we know what they are going through. I believed that if I could know what Mom was going through and not just live by what was happening on the outside, I could do a better job of connecting, a better job of loving.

Many of us are care givers for people suffering from memory loss. The very term care giver implies what we do, give and care. But both the giving and caring can overwhelm us. We can find our limits, become exhausted, battle what seems to be endless emotions. And the struggle can alter our perspective.

We can become overwhelmed by situations and events that are catastrophic. And we can gain a perspective that reduces the catastrophic to repetitive and confusing. In some cases, possibly many, perspective can help us laugh, enjoy, have peace and love amid suffering. That's my goal for this project. To love during suffering, to laugh, enjoy, and connect with the feelings of someone.

When all I see is myself.
When all I feel is me,
the world is very dark.
When another is there,
there is life.
And life is a light in the dark.

SNAPSHOT I

Just because I don't know what you're talking about doesn't mean I don't have an opinion.

Complaining is meaningful to me. It's something I can do.

I didn't complain when I was changing your diaper.

Insight

Being a part of the conversation makes us feel like we belong, that we have value. How can I encourage conversation and not be overly concerned about content?

9

SNAPSHOT 2

Why don't you understand that I don't understand?

Just listen. You don't need to understand or agree, just listen.

You can't control me, but you can love me.

Insight

Most of us listen to respond, not to understand. This creates anxiety in us if the only thing needed is listening. How can I become a better listener?

SNAPSHOT 3

Just because I have a tantrum doesn't mean I don't love you and need you.

When you were a baby I didn't yell at you to calm down.

When you were a baby and sick I didn't get mad at you for not being able to tell me what was wrong.

Insight

Anger often comes out when we feel out of control and overwhelmed. Loving someone can increase that anger as you want so deeply to care for them. How can I control my anger so that my anger is not controlling the people I love?

11

SNAPSHOT 4

The only time when I'm not hurting is when I forget I'm hurting.

You're afraid of the future; I'm afraid of the present.

We cling to life with our memories. When they are gone we feel life is over.

Insight

Pain and fear are a daily part of life. But what happens when we no longer have the ability to hide it? How can I care for a person who will daily face fear and pain?

SNAPSHOT 5

You can't imagine how much courage it takes to live and not be afraid.

Being alone when you're surrounded by people sucks.

I'm scared a lot.

Insight
We seldom see the courage it takes for a person with memory loss to live each day. How can I treat them as courageous and not as needy?

SNAPSHOT 6

It's my life. I'll remember it anyway I want to.

I repeat myself because you didn't listen the last ten times I told you the story.

The memories that I remember are not always the memories I want to remember.

Insight

Correcting people is a normal part of life, of family life. But do we need the negative emotions that often come with hearing a lie? How can I overcome my need to fix what someone is saying?

LOST ON MEMORY LANE

Jeanette Lane. That's Mom's name. She has moved over a hundred and nine times in her life. That is a lot of addresses. This mother of six kids, wife of three husbands, sister to thirteen siblings has had a full life. But most of that is lost now.

15

Mom lives with my sister, but often thinks she is in a home and that Sue is, well she doesn't know who Sue is. "That girl" runs around and comes and goes in Mom's house. Sometimes "that girl" is good. Sometimes "that girl' is a grief. The older more distant memories are the ones mom remembers now. The daily encounters of love and care are lost to her.

I got lost once. Actually, I have been lost a lot, but most of the time it was that, "too proud to ask for directions" lost, or the "I don't want to ask for help with these instructions" lost. YouTube has helped both my pride and my production.

But when I was about 14 years old I was hunting in the Black Hills of South Dakota, and a snow storm came in. I was walking up a 2-mile valley and the plan was to meet our hunting party at the top. When the

16

snow started, it was beautiful. The flakes were like flowers falling from the sky, large and puffy. It was as if you could hear them dropping as they fell by the thousands.

Then the clouds started covering the hillsides. The valley became a gorge and then a ditch as my vision was reduced from miles to feet. And now the wonder that amazed me, paralyzed me. I lost perspective. I lost direction. And as the hours passed by, I lost security, any sense of enjoyment and hope.

I wonder if that is what Mom is facing. That all the things she once saw and knew are now being whited out. That her life is fogged in by clouds and her gaze reduced to her next step. She must feel alone. She might be like me, at the point of being hopeless. That is what happens when we are lost isn't it?

On my adventure I had people who cared for me, people who were looking for me. My ordeal ended when Dad found me. Mom has people looking for her. People care for her. But it doesn't look good. Her life will end with that feeling of lost unless that too is gone.

I called Mom the other day. She was in a panic. She thought the kids were back on the farm and home alone. That she was at "this house" and they wouldn't let her go. She was walking along, and the storm had come in. Her perspective was gone.

I tried to redirect her. In her way she told me she didn't want to talk about the weather; she wanted to know where her kids were. I told her I was her kid. I was Rod, and I was ok.

"I know who you are, but where are the other kids?" Mom directed.

"I love you Mom and wish I was there to give you a hug." I paused. "I'm sorry that you have to go through this. I wish I was closer so that I could give you a hug."

Mom listened, she opened up for a moment and received care. The panic was pushed back for a moment.

When you're lost in a storm sometimes you need a hug. You need someone to pop into view and grab ahold of your heart and squeeze. A moment of love and safety, even if it will be forgotten to the mind it will be embraced by the soul.

I'm mostly lost with Mom these days. I don't know what to do.

I know Mom is feeling lost too. She is often scared. She hides it behind a smile, but I see it. The voices of direction don't seem to help much now. Verbal comfort and conversations end up in those circles of wondering. I don't know if I can stop those; I don't think I can. But I can stop Mom, even if it's only for a moment. I can intersect her life with a hug, an embrace, a touch. And even if I can't help her find her way, I can walk with her awhile.

SNAPSHOT 7

I can feel love even if I can't express it.

Empathy means more than truthfulness, love more than being on time.

It's my reality that has changed, not my love.

Insight

How people behave and our ability to love them are often connected. Unconditional love is hard. How can I grow in unconditional love?

SNAPSHOT 8

If I remembered another story I would tell you that one, but I don't.

I sound like a broken record because I am a broken person.

Insight

We live in a world filled with new. New stories, new technology, new ideas. So how we can be easily troubled by the same old over and over. How can I find peace amid old repetitive stories?

SNAPSHOT 9

Try and figure out what I need from the relationship when you can't figure out what I need in the moment.

Sometimes I just want to connect, to see you smile. I want to get beyond making you feel bad.

Insight

Feeling loved and cared for can greatly help a person who is frustrated or confused. How can I care even if I can't solve the problem?

SNAPSHOT 10

I'm trying one hundred times harder than you think.

If I'm a jerk, you need to deal with it. Chances of me changing are rare.

Please understand that I say things I don't mean, like, "I can take care of myself."

Insight

"You're worthless" may be what they hear when we ask them to try harder. How can we help those who cannot take care of themselves feel like they can?

SNAPSHOT II

Most of what I learned to succeed or survive is worthless now.

Just because it isn't safe or good for me doesn't mean I should be prohibited. I've got to go sometime.

If you choose to keep me safe I may get mad at you.

Insight

Risk and adventure are important to some people. It makes them feel alive. Am I caring for people who needs a little risk in their lives? Who am I trying to protect by keeping them safe?

SNAPSHOT 12

I'm going to give you a piece of my mind as soon as I find it.

Can we laugh awhile? We can fight again later.

Good days give me hope. Even if it is false hope, it is all the hope I have.

Insight

Laughter is good. Even in the worst of times laughter can help with healing and peace. Laugh as much as you can. How can I bring laughter into the lives I care for?

MICKEY

Mickey (my mom's childhood nick name) and I are sitting outside and talking on a calm 106-degree Phoenix day. She is puffing, but not inhaling on a cigarette. At least that is what she tells me. Mom is suffering from dementia. Sometimes she knows it. Sometimes she doesn't.

Mickey is telling me again about the time her dad and mom first met. Actually, they didn't meet, but that is the heart of the story.

Her dad was out of the Marine Corps and hitching train rides across America in search of a job. The remaining sign of his service to our country is his boots, but during the night he took them off, and now they are gone. A smile breaches Mickey's face. The words are coming from her, but I think she sees her dad telling the story to his daughter.

Mom unpacks the story mostly the same, but her illness is taking from her even some of the most loved parts of the narrative. Mom smiles and tells of her dad entering the hotel kitchen where her grandmother worked in Bonesteel, South Dakota. Although she was not born, Mickey sees the images in her mind and joyfully recites how her mom called the hotel, her dad answered the phone, and after a few seconds of conversation told Grandma that he was going to marry her daughter. A New York man and a Bonesteel, South Dakota, woman were wed. Sometimes within three days and at other times three weeks, the details vary.

But what never changes is that each time I heard this story, and I have heard it hundreds of times, Mom is full of that special joy we have when telling someone something exciting for the first time. As I see the glean in her eyes, observe how her mouth half smiles at each telling, hear the lilt in her voice as she is excited to share with me this treasure from her past, her joy in the telling wars against my frustration of hearing it again.

Nowadays most every story Mom tells, she is sharing for the first time. That is what it feels like, that is her reality. Even when the cycle of telling and retelling occurs within seconds, each time the story is told for the first time with the emotions and joy of sharing a wonderfully new and significant tale.

Years ago, Mom watched me. I suppose she felt the joy moms feel in seeing their children grow. I know she also felt the stress of waiting, the wrestling for personal fulfillment, that longing for freedom to run off and do what you want to do. Now it's my turn. My turn to take joy in the present. My turn to put personal fulfillment on hold and use my freedom to listen and love.

In a few moments Mickey is going to tell me that story again. Will I only hear the same repetitive words? Or maybe I will hear the joy she has in the telling, the excitement of sharing for the first time, the treasure offered me as Mom passes on the history of that first encounter.

SNAPSHOT 13

Look at all you do to feel comfortable. I want to feel comfortable too.

There is a time in life when production doesn't determine value.

Quality of life is what you give me when I can't give it to myself.

Insight

What if the desire to be valued, to be valuable doesn't go away, ever? How can I help you feel treasured for who you are and not what you do?

SNAPSHOT 14

If I could change my behavior don't you think I would?

Do what's best for me. That is what I did for you when you were a child. Even if I don't understand or agree, do what's best.

I have a reason to say no to everything. Help me find enough joy to say yes to a few things.

Insight

Change and changing situations involve overcoming fear and learning new things. How do you face your own fears in helping them face theirs?

SNAPSHOT 15

It's not that I don't enjoy life, the joy is just overshadowed by how much I can no longer enjoy.

Hold my hand, touch me. It helps me know you care.

I need something meaningful to do. Even if I do it over and over, if it gives me meaning, let me do it.

Insight

Life is filled with irritations. Many of us use our minds and thought life to get through those moments. What can you do to help someone cope that doesn't require a lot of mental involvement?

SNAPSHOT 16

Complaining is meaningful to me. It's something I can do.

Just because I hate everything doesn't mean I don't waat to enjoy life.

Insight

Bad days might be necessary for meaning. They reveal a struggle is still going on, a fight for life. What can you do to see that the struggles are a fight for life and not just a complaining person?

SNAPSHOT 17

You said I'm safe, but how do I know I'm safe?

You mean I can't remember thirty years of my life?

Let's work together even if I only watch.

Insight

Surrender to the circumstances is hard and seldom feels safe. In what ways do you accept your circumstances and maintain peace?

SNAPSHOT 18

I hate my life sometimes. Sorry, but you get to deal with that too. Sometimes I know it is never going to get better. It overcomes me.

Being realistic requires mental ability. Remember I'm losing my mental ability.

I'm not playing with my food, I'm trying to decide if this is what I'm supposed to eat.

Insight

The loss of simple daily joy can bring about anger and resentment. As a caregiver how are you avoiding daily disappointment and any feelings that your life is over?

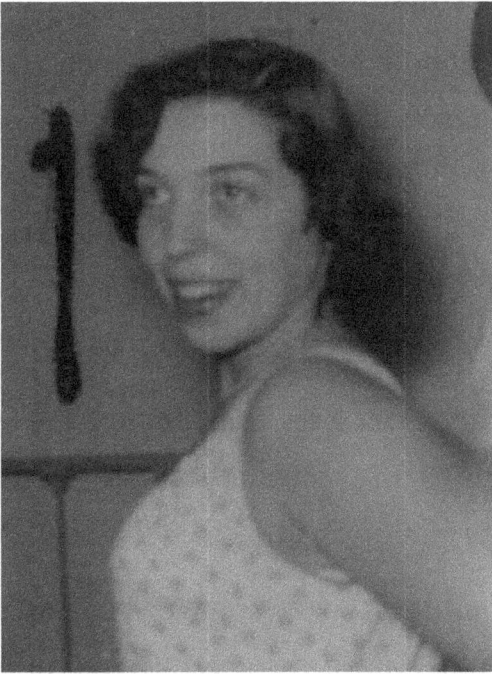

ONE DAY IS LIKE A
THOUSAND YEARS

One day is like a thousand years and a
thousand years like one day. That's from
the Bible, I think.

But I also believe that it may be the thoughts of both a person with dementia and the person who is their care giver. For the person fighting the illness the memories that are moments away feel like a thousand years past. What just happened is difficult, if not impossible to recall.

For the care giver a day may seem to be everlasting. Time seems to stand still. All you have is the present.

The present is all we ever have. The past is over, and the future is not yet. Living in the present is what life is. But when the perspective of the past and the hope for the future are gone, the present becomes a dark and narrow room. It is a prison. It is a spear in the heart. Mom has lost hope for a better future.

She can no longer look forward to smoking a cigarette and having a cup of coffee. She can no longer enjoy the memory of the last cigarette and coffee. I don't know, but I think even her ability to taste is no longer there. We sit and smoke, but its more of an activity than a joy.

You can see it in the way the smoke emanates from her mouth. When the emotions are present, the exhaust of smoke can be violent. It's like the smoke went into the soul, grabbed ahold of some passion and delivers it to the surface so that everyone around has a sign of what is happening in the inner being. At times this release is like a cloud, signaling out a "glad that's over" or a simple "finally."

I've seen a skilled smoker roll the smoke out of his mouth and back into his nose and then back out the mouth again. It's like they are pondering an emotion. "Should I let it out?" "No, keep it in." "Oh, what the hell," and out it comes in a burst of frustration.

Lifeless is the smoke that comes from Mom these days. Not because Mom doesn't have emotions, she does. But she doesn't have an awareness of the past or future that empower the present. It's like she has lost her way and doesn't even know she is lost, only waiting. Like an old steam engine on a track to nowhere, still functional, only lacking a history and a future. Trapped in the present.

I think God is the only one who can live peacefully in the present. It seems to me to be a divine thing. Can any of us be content enough not to need a history or future for significance? I know I'm not like that. I know my mom's not.

I think if I were a smoker I would work hard at doing that out of your mouth and back into your nose thing. I would want to send out the signals that I am sad for my mom, trapped in the moment. I would also want to be honest of the times I am sad for myself, trapped here with her. But with every puff I would also want to remind myself that life is a vapor. It comes and goes quickly. Sometimes others notice our significance. Most of the time we only notice when they are gone.

SNAPSHOT 19

Can you find a way to care for me without asking me how I am all the time?

Give me something I can be in control of, even if it's a box of crackers or a handful of one-dollar bills. Give me some responsibility or at least a gold fish.

I'm depressed, and I can't remember. These are two things not one. Which one can you help me with?

Insight

Questions we can't answer can be irritating. What questions are you asking yourself that might be causing increased anxiety and stress?

SNAPSHOT 20

If I don't know what I want asking me again doesn't help me.

What's wrong with sorting through my stuff every day? What else do I have to do? Should I watch TV even though I don't understand what is going on?

Is it stealing when you take something from yourself and hide it?

Insight

Watching someone do what we consider meaningless activity often produces negative emotions in us. We are production driven. How can I see more activity as play and not work?

SNAPSHOT 21

When you are deceived you don't know you are deceived.

Helping me breathe helps me more than telling me to get a grip.

Next time you yell at me to change my cloths I'm going to yell back. "I forgot how."

Insight

Sometimes we know what is going on, sometimes we don't. Deception is thinking we do, but we do not. How can I make fewer assumptions? Am I OK not being in control?

SNAPSHOT 22

Trusting someone more than you trust yourself is the only way out of deception.

I know what time it is. I just don't remember what it means.

Why is your reality true but mine is not?

Insight

People are raised all their life to have their own perspective, to be their own person. How can I live with conflict and still be a loving, caregiving person?

SNAPSHOT 23

You wonder why I struggle to run a computer. I wonder why you struggle to change a tire, check the oil, wash dishes by hand or call me on the phone.

The old clothes I know are better than the new clothes I do not know.

Insight

"They should be able to" is a trap.
Judging is not as helpful as discernment.
How can we live together without never ending comparison and judgements?

SNAPSHOT 24

Just because I overreact doesn't mean you need to.

When I threaten to leave I'm trying to tell you that I am still valuable, I still count. I hate being nothing.

I repeat myself. Everyday is the same old thing.

Insight

Drama is a part of life and some people get more dramatic because they need to feel alive. How can I tell when I am acting out and when I am acting as I should?

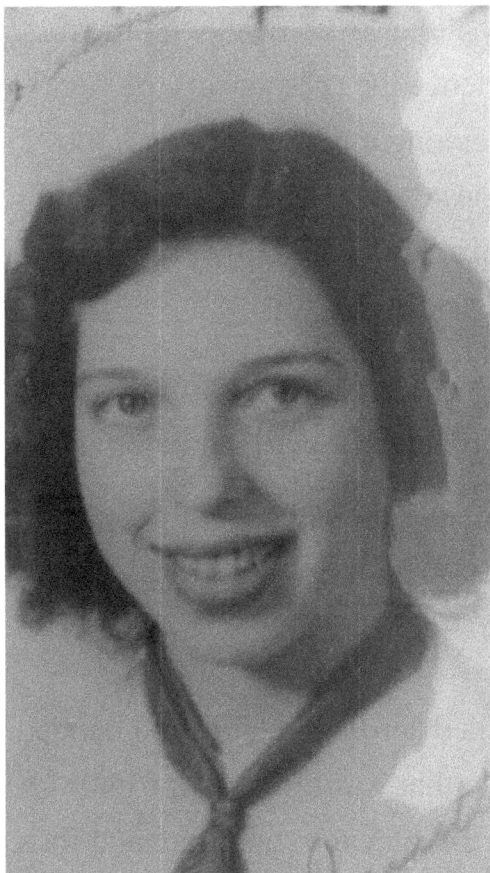

FOGGY

With the changing of the seasons from
summer to fall, fog descends into our

valleys. Our loved ones with memory loss experience the presence of the fog encroaching into their changes too. This fog doesn't just hinder their view of distance, but even things right in front of them can become lost.

Mom sat looking at the table. "Where did it go." "It was just here."

"What are you looking for Mom?" I said.

"The cup, my coffee cup, it was right here." Mom said as she scanned the table.

I reached across the table and handed Mom the cup that was directly in front of her. It was hidden next to her plate and fork. Only 4 items were in front of her, a plate, fork, napkin and the missing coffee cup. But the cup was missing, not from view, but from memory.

Mom had lost the cup in the fog. It was paralyzing her at times now. She knew the word cup, she knew the joy of lifting the cup to her lips and sipping on the coffee. But she, if only for a moment, had lost the image and idea. Mom didn't know what a cup was although she knew she wanted it.

I'm standing now behind her and touch her. The touch helped do what my words could not. Mom felt tenderness and a simple shower of joy flow over her heart. She smiled. Not the self-conscience guilty smile we all have when we are caught in one of life's awkward moments. But that involuntary smile we all have when we feel the presence of love.

When Mom forgets what love is, when all memories of love and life are gone, and only Mom remains, she will remain as an object of love. Like the flower that knows not that the sun is its strength, Mom will know not that she is loved. And yet, what she does not know will strengthen her.

SNAPSHOT 25

If you want to look at me naked, you should have to pay.

Are we married? I think we need to be married for you to touch me there.

How can I embarrass you, I'm the one who can't put on my own clothes?

Insight
Humor often masks fear or disappointment. How can I see the soul in these situations?

SNAPSHOT 26

It's hard to unlearn. I use to be able to cook, drive and go for walks. I know I can, but now I can't.

Don't be like me, ask for help.

All my life I was able to learn. Now I can't.

SNAPSHOT 27

Give me a little space to be grumpy. I'll work it out. Having everything done for me is frustrating.

When the purpose is gone, help me find the pleasure in life.

Faith helps me fight fear, not reason.

Insight

Attitude and emotions come from what we believe, not just what we think. What beliefs am I promoting today?

SNAPSHOT 28

Sometimes I don't remember what you can and cannot eat, I'm embarrassed.

Why do you think I won't try new foods? How many new things do I do everyday? I think this might be the first time I've tried water.

Insight

Life may look repetitive but it might be a never ending series of first time events. How can I live and care for a person experiencing everything for the first time?

SNAPSHOT 29

I don't want you to know that I don't know how to shower or go to the toilet.

Wearing dirty clothes is the result of not knowing the difference between dirty and clean.

I was raised in a materialistic world. When I don't see my stuff, I feel like a failure, like I have nothing.

Insight

Anxiety increases and value decreases when we know that we don't know. How can I communicate value to someone who is not feeling valued?

SNAPSHOT 30

I feel things. It's not just what you say. I see what you are thinking.

I'm not stupid. I'm just losing my mind.

You're calling me a liar, and you want me to trust you.

Insight

Humans have great skill at perception. We understand with the head and the heart. How can I remove the conflict between what I say and what they see?

GIVING

My care givers are God to me. They give
me life and food and joy and purpose. A
newborn child has an inner desire to thrive.
Many times, I don't. But my care givers
give it to me. It is like life is passed on to

me through their living, their listening, their touching and caring.

But also, in their forgiving, their mercy, their patience. The sacrifice of their lives gives me life. When they give peace in exchange for my hostility, that doesn't change my mind, it confronts my heart. Isn't that divine?

Giving, forgiving, sharing, imparting, and giving to me the life that they have, so that I may live too.

SNAPSHOT 31

I know that having mercy on your parent is harder than having mercy on your child.

It's humbling to become a child again, one that needs help to bathe and get dressed.

You are my child, of course I know more than you.

Insight

Learning that the one you are caring for can no longer learn is a difficult change. We are prone to always seek improvement and never decline. What's my plan to deal with a loved one in decline?

SNAPSHOT 32

My nervous reactions that trigger you, help me.

I can't remember if I'm better than I am, or worse.

I don't know how hard I am to be around. I don't know how much you love me and prove it by being here.

> *Insight*
>
> *The feelings of fear and love war against one another. Most people have triggers for fear, but love is not so easily triggered. Often when I feel loved I give love. How can I remind myself to feel love and not just feel the burden of care?*

SNAPSHOT 33

I forget both the bad days and the good.

It means a lot to me when you listen and smile.

A little good is better than no good.

Insight

Sometimes you will need to put the one you are caring for through a difficult situation or day, it simply cannot be avoided. Are you the kind of person who easily feels guilt or shame? How will you deal with your feelings of discomfort for causing theirs?

SNAPSHOT 34

I can't take care of myself, and I feel scared. Even if I say I'm not, I am.

My most sane moments are the most depressing. I become aware of what I am not.

If you need a break, I need a distraction to help me refocus.

Insight

You may be the only source of comfort for the other person. This can be exhausting. Times will come when you need a break, but they need help. How do you know your limits and know when you haven't reached them yet?

SNAPSHOT 35

Will I always feel confused? And if I do, will it always bother you?

Tomorrow will be worse than today, and I know that.

Catastrophic emotions are for when the world comes to an end. My world is coming to an end.

Insight

What we call over-reacting may be appropriate from their perspective. Even when what they perceive is not true, it feels true. You can help someone through the worst day of their life. The question is how?

SNAPSHOT 36

When I feel rushed I lose control, I don't want to, but I do.

You have no right to tell me how to live, when to take a bath, or how to spend my money.

Insight

Years have been spent in the growth of responsibility and being your own person. Now they feel like that independence is not gone, but that it is being taken away. How can I face difficult situations and still honor others?

LAUGHTER

It may have been a true story, or it may have been twelve true stories all packed together. But that didn't matter. What mattered was the smirk on Mom's face. The glint in her eye as she knew what she was saying was a little provocative. The curling of her lips in the telling as she started to laugh as she told the tale.

Mom always had a little dark side, a shadow that enjoyed casting a little shade over another person. Now in remembering the past, true or not, these were moments of expressed joyful emotions for Mom.

One of her favorite tales is about the time she was three or four and her twelve-year-old cousin was with all the kids, playing hide and seek in the yard. Mom, chasing after the older child discovers him peeing on Grandma's rosebush. Expecting to find a new hiding place she found one of grandma's prized plants being defiled.

Into the house mom burst and delighted in exposing the delinquent peer. What joy, these eighty plus years later, does mom have in telling the tale of the provocative plant waterer.

What joy I have in seeing mom laugh. It is like a part of her soul is released anew, if only for a moment. In the sound of laughter, the sound of sorrow is deafened. The smile on her face emerges from her heart, it appears to have the ability to brighten her face, to clear her vision.

"I caught him peeing on grandma's rosebush."

I've heard the tale a hundred times now. And each time it brings back this child's delight in discovery. Each time mom is excited to expose the wrong and enforce the right. Each time Mom delights in seeing a forbidden sight, in calling out an older relative and in being the informant to a loving grandma.

SNAPSHOT 37

Tell me again what love means.

You're lying about me. When you tell people how I behave, you lie.

What is wrong with you? If you love me, you would never say these things about me?

Insight
Truth and love are easily separated.
Work hard at keeping them united, even
in the face of accusation and judgements.
Why do I feel pressured to choose
between being truthful and being loving?

SNAPSHOT 38

Do you know what it's like to think that you did something but didn't?

Yes, I did forget how to button my shirt after I finished the second button.

I honestly think I am fine. I honestly think I can take care of myself. I honestly think I'm not the one deceived. Just as you honestly think I am wrong, I honestly think you are.

> *Insight*
>
> *It seems impossible that someone can forget so fast, but they can. What if you thought remembering was the surprise and forgetting the norm? How would that change your day?*

SNAPSHOT 39

I don't know who you are or why you are in my house, and yet I have stayed calm.

If you can help me be calm and comfortable, you are doing a great job.

Sometimes I know what I am saying hurts you, but I say it anyway.

Insight

Peace is present in a storm not because of the absence of a storm. You're the only peace another may have. How can your ability to weather a situation make today a better day?

SNAPSHOT 40

I pretend to understand. It just works
better.

I forgot who I'm talking to when I pray.

I don't ask you about you because I forgot
what to ask.

Insight

*What is it like to blink your eyes and the
past to be gone? How can a lifelong
joyful memory vanish without a trace? As
a caregiver, your relationship is more
about care and less about shared
experience.*

SNAPSHOT 41

Blind people can't see the stars. I can't see my past.

For you doing the same thing over and over again expecting different results is insanity. For me it is the only way to hang on to what I have.

Rebellion is a planned action. I'm just scared. I didn't plan this.

Insight

The cycles people get trapped in can irritate us. We can feel the frustration of another person, even when they are not feeling it. What is my plan for making peace with repetition?

SNAPSHOT 42

I'm not over-reacting. Do you know how many choices I must make just to get dressed?

I live under a shadow of guilt and shame because I know enough to know I'm not doing well.

I'm feeling powerful emotions, but I don't know what to call them, so I don't know how to tell you what I am feeling.

Insight

For some, fear and anxiety may never go far away. Every act may be a physical and emotional burden. How is your presence making a positive impact on their spirit?

CAREGIVING

My sister Sue is the care giver for my
mom. Sue is an amazing person
masquerading as a normal woman. She
works a full-time job, has a heart full of
dreams and grandkids, maintains her
household alone and cares for Mom. What
I think caring for Mom means is that Sue
gives her life to Mom. That to me is an
amazing thing. For one person to give their
life for another.

Maybe it's a mom thing? Maybe women in
general are wired to be self-giving? But
having the tendencies does not diminish
the honor I have for my sister and all those
who give care to people with memory loss.
For it's not only the sacrifice of time, but
it's the dealing with a lot of stuff.

Sue was loving and caring for Mom, and Mom had no connection to Sue. It was like my sister was laying down her life for a stranger.

Sue was attacked by mom for stealing her money or hiding her glasses. I know this is all a part of the disease. But when you're attacked, even by someone who can't help herself, it sure feels like a real attack. And yet Sue is very enduring and loving. I don't know how she does it.

Sue did a hundred little things that made life for Mom easier. She properly placed the remote, the cigarettes, the dishes, the food all out in ways that allowed Mom to live as independently as possible. It was like Sue was an enabled. She enables Mom to have a little honor and dignity.

I read in a book that God is giving by nature. That giving is something that God does naturally, through creation, through forgiveness, through expression of love for people. If that is true, then my sister, and all care givers, are a little divine.

So how can I give a little back to those who give so much?

SNAPSHOT 43

Medications seem to turn off the little light left in my soul.

Every day I live in fear. I just can't escape.

I act out when I am hurting. I don't know why, I just do.

Insight

Physical and emotional pain is agonizing, but some people would rather have the presence of pain than empty feelings. How can I support their desire rather than enforce my own?

SNAPSHOT 44

I'm a grown person, and I can't even bathe myself. How do you think I feel?

Well you're not the person I remember either.

When I accuse you or get angry at you, remember that I have a disease. I may be difficult, but this illness might make me impossible.

Insight

Conflicts and arguments are a part of life. They will happen disease or no disease. How do I keep myself balanced in the tension of this disease and acceptable behaviors?

SNAPSHOT 45

My life is like being lost in a foreign land and not knowing the language.

The same thing happens when people continue to use a broken toilet or a broken mind. Someone will need to come and clean up the mess.

I am alone. My soul is unable to connect with you.

Insight

We live in a world where broken things are replaced or repaired, but this situation is not going to be fixed. How do I have honor, not frustration for brokenness?

SNAPSHOT 46

I'm reverting back to being a baby.
Sometimes when I smile, it's just gas.

What happens if you forget that I can't
remember?

Quality of life may be a smile, a laugh, or
being allowed to tell the same story over
and over again.

> **Insight**
> *Empathy is not constant, it changes with
> the people and setting. Love and care
> require ongoing adaptation to the
> situations. How is my desire to be
> consistent working against my desire to
> care?*

SNAPSHOT 47

Sometimes when I can't find something right in front of me, I have forgotten what it looks like even though I remember what you call it.

Every time I tell you the same old story, I am telling it for the very first time.

Someone with mental illness is asked to believe the impossible every day. What you see as reality, we see as impossible.

Insight

The obvious is now deceptive. People know when we are displeased and will pretend to know much more than they do. When I am being worn down by the obvious, what is my game plan?

87

SNAPSHOT 48

I'm going to forget what "I love you"
means, aren't I?

When I am in my room, it feels like my
mother hugging me.

If you think my shirt is on wrong, you
should see my underwear.

Insight

*Fear, love and insecurity will be a part
of our lives. From birth till death we all
will face these giants. How you care is
not about helping someone live, but
about helping them be human.*

SNAPSHOT 49

You're an identity thief. You took away all my ID's, credit cards and check book.

Doesn't everyone fear some things that are not real?

Most of the time when I say "OK" I have no idea what will happen next.

Insight

You are going to be accused and attacked. Their perspective demands that what they feel is injustice be addressed. We all respond to real and unwarranted circumstances. How can defending yourself take a back seat to comforting others?

SNAPSHOT 50

I may not remember what I forgot, but I feel it.

Help me be useful even if I'm useless.

I lose stuff because I hide it, so I won't lose it.

Insight

Emotions may linger long after thoughts are gone. A feeling affects behavior as much as understanding something. Do you have both a list of reasons and a list of emotions to use in your caregiving?

SNAPSHOT 51

My heart tells me that someone loves me enough to take care of me. My mind is unable to understand what that looks like.

Sometimes I don't know who I am; how am I supposed to know what I should be doing?

Determine what I need by what I am doing, not saying.

Insight

Body language is a great tool for understanding what someone needs. How can I turn my intuition into understanding?

SNAPSHOT 52

If I can't learn, teaching me won't help.

I don't need to remember what I laughed about, it's OK with me just to laugh.

When you lock stuff up, I feel judged. Help me feel love even if I need stuff locked up.

Insight

Freedom and fun are often seen as the same thing. A good time is getting to do what I want to do. That idea might linger long. How can I help someone have fun without unlimited freedom?

SNAPSHOT 53

I spent my life gathering this stuff, now you say it is unsafe for me. I feel lied to.

I'm grieving the loss of my stuff.

Sincere hugs help.

Insight

People and stuff are two things that make up the memories of our lives. Some will remember people better, others will remember books, homes, cars and other material things. How can I remind myself that a chair might be as meaningful as a child in this condition?

I CORINTHIANS 13 FOR MEMORY LOSS

If you have heard it a thousand times, if it makes no sense to you, love.

If it's not true, if all the facts are mixed up, love.

If you are accused of stealing, of hiding stuff, of taking their stuff, love.

Love is patient and kind, it can wait well and long.

Love doesn't focus on what it could be doing but on what it is doing. Love does not consider potential but persons.

Love does not make things worse needlessly. It does not pay back, does not respond in anger.

Love endures, it suffers. Love hears what is not true and waits. Love believes when all faith is gone. It hopes when life is hopeless.

Good deeds will end. Connection, friendship, family will end. But love does not end. Memories, stories, personal history will all fade away, but love will endure.

Life is a vapor, it is soon over. What we do is soon forgotten. Who we are remains in the hearts of others. The

gifts we gave are forgotten, the gift
we are, remains. Everything ends, but
love goes on.

When we were children life seemed
so different. Now age has made us
wise, and our innocence is lost.
Hopes, dreams, desires have come
and gone. But this endures. Love.

EPILOGUE

A life is lived and then forgotten about by the very one who lived that life. This happens to some of us, not all. And it is hard to go through, hard to watch.

But that "hardness" is the very thing that makes love real. It is the testing of fire, of pressure, those events that paint days and decades outside the box of easy that define love. And what about loving care?

Care, after all, is a word not all that easily given. It is a word that, while simple in notion, is complex in practice. It is the kind of word that we often use and seldom reflect upon the cost or value.

Thank you for opening your life up to love and care for others. Connecting with them, not on their best day, not on their worst day, but through the everyday. Through the grind, the repetition, the slow deterioration and in the exhausting needs for loving care, you are there.

Return to this book and find other ways to restore your soul and gain fresh perspective as you walk beside those leaning on you. And as they lean, lean a little back in. They will feel the pressure and know they are not alone.

Other Books by Rodney A Drury
Available on Amazon

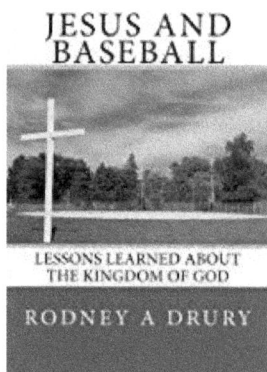

JESUS AND BASEBALL

LESSONS LEARNED ABOUT THE KINGDOM OF GOD

RODNEY A DRURY

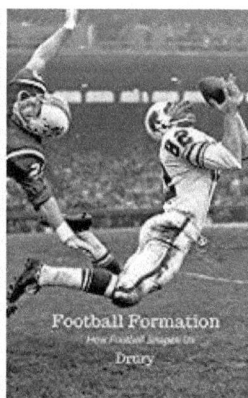

Football Formation

How Football Images Us

Drury

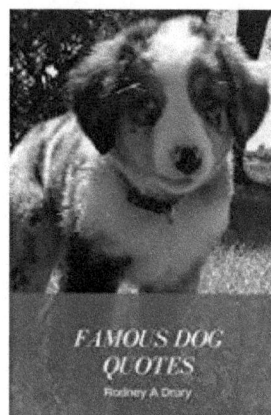

FAMOUS DOG QUOTES

Rodney A Drury

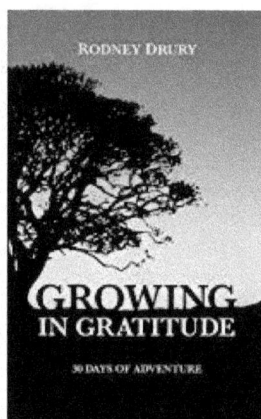

RODNEY DRURY

GROWING IN GRATITUDE

30 DAYS OF ADVENTURE

www.ingramcontent.com/pod-product-compliance
Lightning Source LLC
Chambersburg PA
CBHW070639030426
42337CB00020B/4077